Living WITH Humans
A Canine Perspective On Human Behavior

CHAPS

© Chaps 2018

Print ISBN: 978-1-54394-652-9

eBook ISBN: 978-1-54394-653-6

Registration Number TXu-102-246

All rights reserved. This book or any portion thereof may not be reproduced or used in any manner whatsoever without the express written permission of the publisher except for the use of brief quotations in a book review.

TABLE OF CONTENTS

PROLOGUE xi
CHAPTER 1 3
CHAPTER 2 15
CHAPTER 3 23
CHAPTER 4 31
CHAPTER 5 45
CHAPTER 6 53
CHAPTER 7 61
CHAPTER 8 69
CHAPTER 9 75
CHAPTER 10 81
CHAPTER 11 89
CHAPTER 12 95
EPILOGUE 101

*Dedicated to all humans that love, appreciate and respect the animals that share life on this planet
Especially my mother*

PROLOGUE

PROLOGUE

My name is Chaps and I am a member of the genus Canis. In other words, I am a dog.

I decided to write my memoir as a gift to my family. It was after my 15th birthday party in January of 2016. I realize that I have a very full and special life. I wanted them to know how much I have appreciated all the life experiences they make possible.

So you are probably wondering how does a dog write his memoir. I am a very lucky boy.

I have a scribe that I communicate with to get my thoughts down on paper. I do not have thumbs or the dexterity to write. So I have to rely on a human to scribe for me. We can read each other's thoughts. Not all of the time but when we both focus on the subject matter it works.

While writing my memoir, we both had many frustrating hours. Neither of us wanted to go through the exercise again. However as I was writing my memoir, I realized I had more to say that did not necessarily fit in a memoir.

So I decided, that I would wait for the right moment to let my scribe know that no matter how painful it would be, it was extremely important to me to communicate to humans how they are perceived by this member of the genus Canis.

I did not get an enthusiastic response to pursue this project. I have learned that persistence pays off and I kept at it until my scribe gave in to my request. I used my "anything to shut you up routine".

Now you are probably thinking there is no way a dog can communicate with words humans understand absolutely no way. You are 100% correct. I cannot convey my thoughts using the words that humans will understand. I however, can get my message across and my scribe puts it into words that are understandable to humans. It is like trying to get directions in a country where you do not understand the language. Eventually, if one tries hard enough more often than not one can get the message across.

So perhaps I should try to explain the process we go through. First I have to get my scribe into the office and at the computer. This in and of itself is not an easy task. Getting this human's attention and persuading her that it is important can take awhile. Then I usually lie in my bed and begin to transmit my thoughts. When I want to make an extremely important point I lie down on the floor right next to the computer.

I let the scribe know what I am thinking. Somehow and I do not know exactly how, my scribe types my thoughts or transmissions into the words that humans understand. My scribe reads back to me what has been typed and if it is what I am trying to communicate I give my "yes" sign. If it is not and more often than not this happens then I give my "no" sign and usually grunt in frustration. Like I said this is not a pleasant exercise. However, I hope it is one that is worthwhile.

I think a little background is in order. I was blessed to be a part of a special family. When I was 9 weeks old I was placed with this new family. I moved away from my mother, siblings and the people I knew and relied on for my first 9 weeks.

I was scared. I mean really scared, as we drove off not knowing what lie ahead. I knew that I was going to have to learn how to survive in a world controlled by humans. No longer could I look to my mother for food, comfort and protection. I would have to find new ways to take care and entertain myself.

As I look back on my puppy days, I reflect on how much I have experienced. More importantly, how much I have learned about my life interacting with humans. So this is my attempt to share what I have experienced during my life with humans and have observed about their behavior towards the animal kingdom and to each other.

For those of you willing to be open to perhaps a different perspective, this is for you.

CHAPTER 1

"Bad human communication leaves us less room to grow"

Rowan Williams

CHAPTER 1

I had been with my family about a month when one Saturday a young woman named Dagny came to the house. She seemed nice enough when I first met her but unbeknownst to me at the time she was there to train me. Even though I was very young she thought I was ready to be trained.

So began my formal training. We went through sit, down, stay, come and heel. The training was totally focused on my responding to human commands. I knew that was necessary to maintain discipline and harmony in the house. However, what it failed to cover was the other side of the relationship.

I needed to communicate my needs to them. They had to know when I was hungry and when I had to go out to tend to myself. For me communication was key to surviving with humans. Even at 4 months old I knew that I was going to have to figure this out for myself since I could not hire a trainer to come in and train them.

I looked for clues on how to achieve my goals. I needed to develop a road map to understand how best to communicate with humans. I knew that this was not going to be an easy task but a critical one if I was going to make it in my new environment.

An early clue happened on our way home from the place I was born. We stopped and Nancy got out of the car and I admit I was scared because I realized that I had been taken from the only place that I knew. Just think of how you might feel if all of a sudden you woke up one morning and your normal routine started out like every other day of your short life and all of a sudden a couple of people come into the house and you play with them for awhile and before you know it you are in a car heading out of the driveway.

No one informed me that I was leaving the only home I knew and these two strangers were going to be responsible for me. No one asked me if I even liked these two. I did not know what was happening to me.

After driving for a very long time, you have to understand I was just 9 weeks old and had never been in a car and all of a sudden I was in this thing with two strangers that had my life in their hands. They seemed nice enough and I did not feel like I was in danger but this was all too new for me.

I really panicked when the car stopped and I saw one of them get out of the car. I looked out the window and Nancy looked at me and said "it's ok buddy, I'm just getting gas for the car". It was like she could read my mind. She was communicating with me. I felt a lot better. I knew that I would be OK and secure. I could feel the love and caring from Carol on the very long trip to my new home. She was definitely the nurturer in the family but she had to understand my needs.

It seems to me that humans figure they know everything there is on how to take care of animals. There are books and TV shows that lay out the best ways to train animals. They hire trainers or go to obedience classes. In my humble opinion, they totally miss the boat because like my training with Dagny they totally focus on responding to human commands.

The focus is not on communicating but limited to what the human wants the animal to do. I was not going to let my relationship with my family be a one way street. If I was going to survive being controlled by humans it was going to be a two way street. So I developed a plan.

Since I had been with my new family for about a month I had begun to scope out who was who in the family. Carol was the best she spoiled me from the minute I got into the car. She tended to my needs the best she could. I had to find a way to communicate my needs to her. Nancy was the analytical one in the family and until I got there the Alpha member. She was the one I felt I could communicate with more easily. She seemed to know that communication was important in this relationship as well.

So my plan was to train Nancy first. To start she needed my code for "yes" and "no". I was surpised that it did not take her long to catch on. Like I said Nancy is very intense and analytical, so it was no wonder that one day she came home with this book titled "Animals in Translation".

She took the initiative to try to learn to communicate with me. Evidently the book explains how animals process information and how to understand the cues they give to people if the person is open to understanding them. I heard her tell many people in my early days about this book and how it was helping my family to communicate with me.

In no time my family knew that if they asked me a question and the answer was yes I would raise my paw and if the answer was no I would turn my head away from them. Needless, to say this was the start of our two way communication.

If I needed to go out and tend to myself. I would stand at the door. If they were not in the area I would either go get them and take them to the door or I would use my I have to go out sound. When I am hungry I lick my chops. Sometimes I go to the kitchen and either stand at the oven or refrigerator. This all took time, patience and consistency.

We were beginning to understand that we had to be sensitive to each others needs through a series of established cues. On my end when they said "sit" I would sit. I did have a bit of a problem with the "come" command when I did not want to come. However, I would do my best to comply. This was the beginning of our two way communication relationship.

I think they were beginning to see the benefits of communication and not just having me respond to commands. Our relationship with each other began to evolve in a number of ways.

Trust me, humans hop to when you let them know that you have to tend to yourself. Humans do not like it when dogs tend to themselves in the house. Of course they do little to invent a place or a gizmo for us to use to tend to ourselves inside and train us to use it.

So for some reason, which I fail to understand when an accident does occur it is always "bad boy" or "bad girl" like it is always our fault that the human was not paying attention or just ignore any cues that we may give. Classic example of lack of communication.

I have a hard time understanding why humans think we can go and tend to ourselves on command. So what normally happens is they take us or let us out when it is convenient for them and not necessarily when mother nature hits us.

Humans tend to themselves when they choose and at a place called a toilet. Some dogs can go out through what is called a doggy door and cats have litter boxes but for the rest of us it helps to develop the communication with the family to keep everyone happy.

My code system was working well but it was just step one in my two way street training program. Bad or inconsistent communication on both sides was going to make life a lot harder. I had to be consistent with my cues and sounds and they needed to be consistent with their commands and actions. Communication without consistency was going to be a nightmare and extremely frustrating for all involved.

I realized that one of the reasons that Nancy bought the book "Animals in Translation" was because she thought that I was incredibly smart. She kept telling Carol that she could not get over how much I understood. So in my own way I needed to let her know she was right I am smart. The more that I could encourage these two to communicate with me the easier it was going to be for me to train them. More importantly as I learned over time it was the catalyst for a stronger relationsip.

For example, I had this great pool I loved to go outside and play in. Since I could not go out as much as I wanted Nancy started spelling POOL instead of saying it. After a week or so I figured out that POOL and pool were the same thing. I realized it was up to me to let this human know that given the opportunity we animals are a lot smarter than we are given credit. I also figured out the more I let them know in my own way what I liked and what I didn't like the more complete both our lives would be.

I wanted to let them know that not only could I be trained I could also be educated. Yes, I said educated. I will make my case for this concept later but I do believe it starts with communication and being exposed to different types of experiences.

Since step one was working with my family, I had to figure out how to communicate with less understanding humans. At the time, I did not realize how hard the next step was going to be. I was still a young pup. I had a lot to learn myself. I guess being naïve at an early age is not unusual for humans as well as this young pup. I thought I could conquer any and all obstacles. I craved learning new things and experiencing new adventures.

My family is active and I experience all kinds of things. Like I said I was blessed to be in a family that treated me as an equal. They speak to me as if I am human. In the beginning I have to admit most of the time I did not totally understand what they were saying. I tried to put the words together with what took place immediately after they spoke to me.

So for instance, when asked if I wanted to go for a walk in the park. I knew that we would have to get in the car to get to the park as opposed to "do you want to go for a walk" which meant we would walk around the neighborhood. I would also let them know if I did not want to walk in the neighborhood by going to the door to the garage. It was my way of letting them know on that particular day I wanted to go to the park.

As I got older, I realized that even at an early age they gave me choices. Their communcation with me usually started with phrases "do you want..." or "do you need to". I have come to learn that this is not the norm for humans relating to their "pets" as we are often referred. I was fortunate to have the kind of upbringing that fostered communication between the two species.

As a result, I had no reason to rebel. I did not chew or destroy things. They made sure I stayed engaged. In my own way I let them know that I appreciated their inclusion in their lives by not misbehaving much. I of course like any puppy would get into a certain amount of trouble but more often than not because I was still trying to establish boundaries between good behavior and bad.

So often misbehavior is the result of either looking for attention, frustration or boredom. I am sure there are many other reasons but for the most part it is a way to get human attention.

I was trying very hard to learn how humans communicate and translate it back to a canine understanding of the experience. This took time, patience and a few mistakes along the way. Actually, a lot of mistakes along the way. Trust me, I did not understand a lot of what was happening around me. I would try to communicate and more often than not in the beginning humans including my family had no clue what I was trying to communicate. However, over time persistence paid off.

I would listen to humans talk and watch how they acted towards me and with each other. Some days I thought I got it, I understand humans and the next day I knew I had no clue. I realized that life with humans was going to be complicated.

I was developing from a very young pup to a young canine. In my first year, I learned a lot about myself. I liked to experience new things. A walk or more often a good run on the beach and exploring the rocks at the beach. I loved experiencing life outside the house.

I got to go hiking and kyaking. With the help of a puppy knapsack, I had the best seat in the house on our bike rides. One gets a very different perspective seeing your surroundings 5 feet off the ground. I found myself really liking being a part of a human family. I tend to be curious by nature and this family provided me a myriad of experinces to feed my curisosity and quest to learn. It also got me into a bit of trouble along the way.

My daily walks were a great way to explore new things. These forms of entertainment were particularly special because I got to do them with my family and at the same time got great pleaure from all of the new sights and especially the smells. It was an eye opener to see how humans experience events differed from mine.

One example is watching a beautiful sunset at the beach. I find it unbelievably breath taking. The smells are incredible and the sound of the waves calming. For me, a beautiful sunset is Nirvana. Over the years, I have met a few humans that feel about sunsets the way I do. For the most part, they usually use it as a way to meet and talk. I couldn't help but feel sorry for them because they missed out on such a beautiful experience.

On our kyak rides I would perch on the bow being very quiet not to disturb the birds particluarly the Osprey in their nests. The smells were unbelievable and the sounds of the birds communication a bit mind boggling.

Biking was aways a blast because heads turned when people realized there was a dog and not a baby in the knapsack. I found this very funny and quite interesting since at the time I thought all of this was normal. Every canine that lived in a family and not in a pack got to do all the things I was getting to do. As I got older I found that my life was not necessarily the norm.

What I found early on is that humans talk a lot. I figured this was their main method of communication. So while I struggled with trying to communicate with humans, it became apparent that in order to function in a human's world I had to understand the language humans used to communicate with me and with each other. It was one of my missing links to accomplish my goal of co-habitating in a human controlled world. I needed to learn and appreciate this thing called language.

CHAPTER 2

"A different Language is a different Vision of Life"

― · ―

Frederico Fellini

CHAPTER 2

In the canine world we communicate with each other very differently than humans do. We rely on sight, scent and instinct. For the most part we communicate with each other through our thoughts. If we have to make a point we take it up a notch. We growl to send a warning if we feel threatened and wag our tails when we are happy or nervous. If humans are in sync with us they will see that we smile when we are very happy or have been praised for doing good.

I have developed a system of sounds and barks to let my family know what I am trying to communicate. For instance, when I am not happy with them I have a bark that lets them know they are in trouble with me. I make these sounds when they return to the house after being out late or forget to turn on the lights if they are going to be gone after dark.

Sometimes I have resorted to other ways to speak to my family. For instance, I like to spend time in my beds. I also like to have a clean bed. So when my bed is not quite to my liking, I lay along side of my bed instead of in it and my message is understood loud and clear. Once washed I am back in the bed in a nano second.

Now when I walk with Carol I have my friendly "have a good day" bark for other humans passing by. Then there is my I have to go out and tend to myself sound. Nancy says it definitely gets the message across that I am in distress. I have found that people do respond to my sounds. If I am visiting with someone during a walk they tend to talk back to me. We are speaking different languages but we get our message across.

It takes awhile to appreciate the nuances of the tones but when they do, it works out great. I just had to be consistent with the sounds and what I was trying to communicate. I find that humans love it when they feel like they are successfully communicating with me. A big smile and some comment like he's talking to me is the normal response I get.

If this sounds odd just think of a human trying to communicate with someone who does not speak the same language. The major difference being that humans expect another human to figure out what they are trying to communicate. More often than not this is not the case with animals.

Given that humans like to talk, I began to take advantage of venues where humans would talk a lot. On our walks we would always stop so that my family could visit with other humans who were sometimes walking their dogs as well. Over time some of these canines and I have become friends.

My best buddies and I met this way. While we take in all the great smells and experience life and nature our humans enjoy themselves talking to each other. I knew if I was going to grow I had to figure out not only what they were saying to me but as important what they were saying to each other.

The other thing that I learned early on was that not all humans speak or understand the same language. I found this fascinating. My family has friends that do not speak the language that they speak. My family speaks a language called English. The lady that cleans our house speaks Spanish. We have a good friend that speaks German. What I found amazing was no matter what language that they speak to me in I can for the most part understand what they are saying to me.

For me it is about the vibe I get. The tone that is used to talk to me and the actions they take when they are speaking to me. It takes the whole package for me to be able to understand the message. This is particularly true when I try to put together concepts.

My family has a very good friend from Hamburg Germany. Britta use to spend a lot of time in the winter in Naples Florida. She would sit on the floor and play with me. She always spoke to me in German. Now I am not suggesting that I can understand German but I was able to put the whole package together and more often than not respond correctly to what she was asking me to do. When I did respond to her she would throw her head back and laugh and tell my family how smart I was. I loved it because she had the best laugh.

Over the years I have built an impressive vocabulary if I do say so myself. I have worked very hard to understand the way humans behave by how they use language and the actions that follow. I have learned to put the words that are spoken together with these actions to form concepts. For me this was critical to survive and thrive in life.

In my memoir, I talk about my earliest impressions of human behavior. I discuss how as a young pup I noticed that human liked to talk a lot and they like to celebrate this thing call "Holidays" with each other. I noticed that they give each other "gifts".

Now it is no secret that I love to get gifts. One of the first things I let my family know was my fondness for presents. I received great presents when I first joined my family. All of our family and friends weclomed me into the family with presents. I had lots of toys to play with and to this day really enjoy playing with my toys.

I was exposed to this thing called "shopping". I found out a lot about humans shopping. Now this is one of the human behaviors I really like. We do not exchange gifts or go shopping in the canine world. At least not in the same context as humans. I have friends that brought canine presents to their family. Somehow, their family did not really appreciate the mice, rabbits and other assorted prey they hunted. I am not a hunter. It is not in my DNA or stated in another way my breed is not inclined to hunt.

My family would some times take me shopping. For me it was a good way to better understand human behavior. In my quest to understand communication and language shopping provided a great learning experience. Now I got to go in what is referred to as "Pet Friendly" stores. On occasion, I would pick out the presents myself.

I would be given a choice of items and if I liked the choice I would put my paw up for my "yes" and if I did not like the choice I would turn my head for my "no". At first the store clerk would look at my owner like she was either totally crazy or highly eccentric.

However, I learned that once that clerk realized that I was making the decision on the purchase the attitude towards me changed significantly. All of a sudden they paid attention to me. I became their customer. I was making progress on my plan to participate in a human controlled world.

A classic example of this is during a Christmas shopping trip to a store in our home town that is pet friendly. We were looking for a black v-neck cashmere sweater. At first all the communication was directed between the two humans. This behaviour was quite typical.

The very pleasant sales lady laid four black v-neck sweaters on the counter. Nancy to her credit looked at me and asked "do you like this one" and pointed to the first sweater.

I gave her my no sign and we moved to the next and again I gave my no sign until we got to the last sweater and I gave my yes sign.

The sales lady watched all of this and asked if I was sure that I wanted the fourth sweater and again I said yes but this time to her. She looked at me and told me I had excellent taste. She then asked if I wanted to look at anything else. Indeed I did, we moved over to the Jewerly area to look for some errings. At this point, the communication moved from being just between the two humans to the sale lady and me with a bit of interpetation from Nancy.

I was beginning to be able to communicate in a human controlled world but I was a long way from putting all of the pieces of the puzzle together.

Still I was missing a link to understanding how to thrive in a human controlled world. So far, I knew that communication was key and the key to communication was understanding language. I was learning that the more that I understood the language the better I could communicate with humans. What I was missing was Knowledge.

CHAPTER 3

"The good life is inspired by love and guided by knowledge"

Bertrand Russell

CHAPTER 3

I came to understand that all species for the most part gain knowledge from their personal experiences. As a young pup in a new environment, I was experiencing life with a new family. Each day brought new experiences and with each new experience new knowledge. I was less than six months old and life was great. I was gaining knowledge and I didn't even know it.

While writing my memoir, I looked back at all my experiences and know today that those experiences are what shaped my view of the world and more importantly of humans. During my first six months, I thought all humans were pretty cool. My family was terrific. They took care of all of my needs and exposed me to all kinds of new things. Everyone that I came into contact with me treated me with a lot of love and affection. Even those humans that are not normally fond of animals were kind. All I knew was love. My perspective on life and humans only being good changed on September 11th 2001.

On this day I learned that life was not all fun and games. There was a side to humans that I had no idea existed. We were getting ready to go to the city when the phone rang. Nancy turned on this thing called a "TV". I did not know what was going on but the vibes that I picked up let me know it was not good.

For the next few days everyone was glum. I learned during this time that humans get a lot of their information from the TV. I would be lying if I told you that I understood what was going on but I did learn that some humans are not good.

Like I said, my entire life (all of six months), I had only experienced good. I had no idea about the bad things in the world. My view of the world had been limited and very one sided. I now sat with my family and watched people crying and emotions I did not know existed. Some people were angry and some were scared.

I have to admit I was scared. I had never seen Carol cry before. Nancy who tends to be intense in the best of times was down right worried. They both let me know that we were safe. This life experience I could have done with out but I learned that in fact this is life. From this moment, I knew to survive in this world I was going to have to find a way to gain knowledge. I came to understand that there is more behavior like what we experienced on this dreadful day than one would like to admit.

I started to watch and listen to this thing called TV. I must admit that I have probably learned more about humans watching TV than anything else. It is right up there with life experience. In some ways it was greater and much more expansive than my life experiences. I was able to pick up so many concepts and opinions on human behavior. It was amazing how much one can learn by watching TV.

Depending on what was on the TV, I was able to expand my knowledge base beyond just my own life experiences. This vehicle to learning combined communication, language and knowledge into one forum. I had no control over what I watched. Some times I would just sit with my family while they watched TV.

Nancy believed that animals processed information differently than humans. I suspect she picked this notion up in books like "Animals in Translation". So when my family left me home by myself they would leave the TV on for me. Most of the time the History or Discovery channel would be the channel of choice. Somehow, I think they thought it would keep me entertained. I am not sure they realized I found this a great vehicle to gain the knowledge I felt I needed to make it in their world. I wanted it to be our world.

I learned so much by watching TV. I learned a great deal about the animal kingdom of which I am a member. I learned how animals as we are referred to by humans live among themselves and how they are treated or should I say a mistreated more often than not by humans.

I was particularly intrigued by the intelligence of chimps and gorillas. The one show that I thought crystalized the depth of animal intelligence and behavior was a documentary on elephants. Not only are elephants utilitarian, intelligent more importantly the emotions they exhibit parallel many in the animal kingdom and human emotions as well.

I feel very strongly that humans underestimate the depth of emotion we experience. Perhaps, more recently the emotional aspect of us in the animal kingdom is being slowly acknowledged and to some extent appreciated by humans that live with us day to day.

TV documentaries like the one on Elephants give me hope that some day we in the animal kingdom will be better understood and our potential fully utilized to make the world we all live in a better place. I see it more in the last few years or maybe I just am gaining enough knowledge to appreciate that our station in life is beginning to reflect who we are and what we can be.

For me the big question is if humans know that we are intelligent if properly trained or better yet educated, why do so many suppress our potential? Why do so many humans treat us in ways that are oppressive and counter productive. Today there are scientific studies that support our potential and concrete experiences that validate our potential. Still there are many humans that refuse to acknowledge we have much to offer for one reason or another.

So for me gaining knowledge came in several forms. Life experiences and watching TV were the most expansive but being read to was my favorite. I learned that humans gain knowledge by doing this thing called "reading". People read books for many reasons. One of the reasons people read is for enjoyment. For me it was great to have my family read out loud to me. This normally happened on a rainy or snowy day. Snuggled on the couch. I learned new things from being read to. Honestly, I did really like snuggle time as well.

Over the years I have been able to build on my communication and language skills to enhance my knowledge of a world controlled by humans. I am not suggesting that I am able to achieve the level of sophistication of the human species but I can share a perspective that may differ from many that have been put out there by humans.

In any event, the chapters that follow are intended to simply share with you the observations of human behavior that I have observed over my long and blessed life. So I submit these observations and thoughts from a different perspective, my canine perspective.

CHAPTER 4

"Human behavior flows from three main sources: desire, emotion and knowledge"

Plato

CHAPTER 4

As I mentioned earlier, I learned a great deal by watching TV. The programming on many of the educational shows enabled me to learn about animal and human interaction beyond my own experiences.

A lesson I learned is not to generalize. The fact of life is that there is good and bad in every species. My first realization of this came on 9/11. What I experienced during the months after 9/11 was very different from my carefree life with my family. This was a lesson that I had to remind myself of many times over the years. It is very easy to generalize. So I do try not to generalize however when I feel that behavior is overwhelmingly flawed I have to make my feelings known to whoever will listen to me.

As a young pup I had a lot of questions about humans. I mean a lot of questions. Just think one day you are eating off your mother's nipple and she cares for you and then all of a sudden you are in a car in my instance with two strange humans. Nine weeks old and I had to think who are these people and how am I going to survive. My instincts kicked in, I kept asking myself why I was placed with humans and not other dogs?

Living in a world controlled by canines could be simpler. I knew how to communicate with other canines. In the canine world we have a pecking order for the most part we respect. Our lives are to some extent controlled by our pecking order. This order enables us to sustain ourselves.

There is socialization in the pack. For the most part we live in harmony. Most threats to our lives come from external factors. Much like humans we guard our space and to a large extent each other. As I have learned, life in a human environment is somewhat similar in that members of the pack come in and out of ones life a lot like humans relationships. There is a deep desire to protect those in our pack. We procreate to maintain the strength of the pack. As pups depending on our role in the pack we have to learn to learn to hunt for food and to protect ourselves from external threats and now and again even threats within the pack itself. Honing our instincts is a top priority. Our survival depends on our ability to cohabitate with each other. In this regard life can be a lot harder than a life in a human family. The major difference is that we know how to communicate with each other and in many ways we do not complicate life. Yes, in many ways it can be more dangerous living in the wild but it is also much less complicated.

However my destiny was to live in a human controlled world. One of the benefits is that I did not have to worry about my care and food living with humans. I was also lucky to be part of a family that enabled me to have many experiences, meet many people and travel to many places. I was one of the lucky ones.

I was not going to be a part of a pack. I was going to be part of a family. I was going to have to use all of the traits needed to survive in pack life but I was going to use them differently to survive in a human family.

I had not been born in the wild but in a human home. My mother cared for me. She provided my nourishment and she looked after me. I noticed she was fed and tended to by humans. As I got older humans took over more of my care. It seemed my destiny in this world was to live in a world that was human oriented.

I learned from the outset that the people I would grow to love, my family, had a strong desire to make sure that I had a full and happy life. I had strong desire to not let them down. I was going to make them proud of me. I think it was the strong desire that enabled us to bond from the very beginning.

Desire is very important to humans. Over the years I have learned that desire can be a good thing or it can lead to some very bad things happening. Nonetheless, humans and believe it or not the animal kingdom members are all impacted by desire.

Knowing that my life would be in a human controlled world, I asked myself why would a human want to have a dog in their life? More importantly, how do they value us and what do we add to their lives?

Over time I came to realize that there are many reasons why humans want dogs or more broadly animals in their lives. In my case, I was part of a breeding program. My parents were show dogs. I provided income to this human family. I was sold to a family for money. For them I was considered an asset. That is not to mean that they were not kind. They treated all of us very well. My breeder as they are referred to was very particular as to where and with whom we would spend our lives.

I was lucky. Not all dog breeders are kind. Many are down right criminals. I watched a TV program on puppy farms that made me sick to my stomach. I could not stop thinking about those poor pups. More often than not this thing called "Greed" causes misery. These breeders are driven by greed and the only value they have for the animals is what they can be sold for. The pups are not nourished properly or taught manners. They are shipped in horrible conditions and sold to puppy stores of one kind or another.

I had a hard time with this buying and selling of animals. I have to admit it did lower my opinion on humans. To make matters worse one night I watched a documentary where humans were selling other humans called slaves. For weeks after that I had no use for humans. For me it is fine to buy or sell cars, houses, and other non-living items but other humans and animals no way.

The good news is that it is no longer legal to buy or sell humans or to mistreat them. The bad news is that it is still legal to buy and sell animals. Although, progress has been made. There are laws that protect animals against human cruelty.

A good first step, but more has to be done to protect the abuse to animals. There are many groups that are committed to protecting animals and their rights. These dedicated individuals have experience the fulfillment one can experience with an animal in their life. I wondered why more humans did not think this way.

Upon further thought I realized that it is not just animals that some humans have no regard for but many times they have no regard for other humans. These human beings have little desire to make the effort to better their relationships. Their desire is driven by greed.

Thankfully, not all humans are driven by greed. Many humans feel the same way I do and often seek out animals that have been abused and give them loving homes and good lives. I have a tremendous amount of respect for these individuals.

There are many other reasons humans want an animal in their lives. A very important reason is utilitarian.

Within our species there are a number of what humans call "breeds". Dogs come in all sizes and colors. Some breeds are especially good at different jobs. There are breeds that help herd cattle and assist hunters. Other breeds are trained to save lives. Not unlike humans we all want a purpose in life. Many animal species are happiest when they know they have a job. For them a job is a purpose. I think that is true for all of us. In a pack we have a defined role. In a human dominated environment it can be harder to find ones purpose.

Humans have identified areas where we can perform functions better than they can. For instance, a canine's keen sense of smell has aided in disaster recoveries. On 9/11, within hours after the attack, rescue dogs were right there with the human first responders looking for survivors and recovering those that had not. My canine brethren worked tirelessly to do their job. Watching the teams of humans and canines working together for a common cause was a very proud moment for me. Today many police departments have K-9 units that assist in finding missing persons and escaped criminals. The successes these teams have accomplished are undeniable.

Humans have a propensity to fight with each other in ways unimaginable in the animal kingdom. If we fight with each other we do it hand to hand so to speak. Humans devise all kinds of devices to fight their battles.

In what humans refer to as the "military" canines play an integral role in sniffing out IEDs one of the devices used by the enemy to kill our servicemen and women. Together with their military brethren they go out and patrol searching for these devices. This is another example of the potential that can be accomplished if humans would optimize the potential within the animal world in an equal partnership.

Humans that understand that combining the strength of the canine scent and the human dexterity can avert many casualties. It took humans willing to communicate in partnership with their canine counterpart to create a successful operation. It took hours of learning two-way communication to develop in each case. This is an incredibly strong and powerful relationship. Each would gladly give their life for the other.

The common thread in each of these partnerships is desire. A desire so strong, it drives a willingness to commit. To commit to consistent communication on the part of the human and a willingness to learn and desire to achieve the goal on the part of us animals. Each of these canines has a purpose in life that requires a human counterpart. For us, our greatest desire is to please the human that we interact with every day.

Like the keen sense of smell we also have a sensitive instinct. In the wild, instinct is critical to survival. To survive we have to use all of our senses at a very high level. In a domesticated environment instinct enables us to alert humans to potential danger. Many humans have survived catastrophic situations because they heeded the animals warning even when no apparent danger seemed eminent.

These relationships are evident everyday. On any given day whether in a newspaper or on the TV a story will detail the heroic effort that some animal performed to save a life. Recognition of the potential partnerships in a variety of areas is beginning to resonate with many humans.

The great thing is that an animal's ability to assist humans in their world is more and more accepted in everyday life. For example, dogs are trained to be seeing -eye companions for the blind. The training and devotion it takes for this partnership is driven by the deep desire of the human to trust that his partner will protect him or her as they go about a daily normal routine.

Therapy dogs have enabled many humans to survive stressful situations. These talented animals enable humans to deal with the issues that no medicine or human therapist can heal.

At least one canine thinks he can write a piece on his perspective on human behavior and has persuaded his human scribe to partner with him on this endeavor.

We tend to protect those humans that we live with or in some cases work with. I guess those of us that are domesticated tend to think of our human family as our pack.

However let me state here that being part of a family and trying to understand their desires and deal with their emotions is much more difficult than cohabitating in a pack.

Humans have many emotions that we in a domesticated environment must learn to understand. When some one in my family is sick or sad, I do my best to comfort them. I pick up on the change in their emotion. I put aside my needs or desires to focus totally on the their issue.

Some Human emotions are totally puzzling to our way of thinking. Humans have been known to take out their bad day on the dog. I have heard on TV someone say "I am going home and kick the dog". Now let's think about that for a moment.

I have already stated that what brings the most pleasure to us is to please. So when you come home after a bad day in the office or wherever we greet you with lots of love and affection. We are excited to see you and the thought that all you want to do is kick the dog just doesn't make any logical sense.

We can sense your emotions. We know when you are feeling bad and when you are ill. For the most part given the opportunity we are most likely the best medicine for what ails you. It really works well when the communication is a two way street.

For those humans that have the commitment to communicate with us and live in harmony with us, they know that we too have emotions.

When my best buddy passed on I was in another state and yet I knew what had happened. I cried and was very upset. My family thought that I did not feel well physically but that was not the problem. I would never see or experience the good times we had again. I knew he was in a better place but I could not help feeling sorry for myself.

I kept trying to herd my family to the couch. I knew if I could get them to the couch one of them would discover the real reason I was not myself. All I had to do was to get one of them to pick up that thing they call an iPad. Indeed that is exactly what happened. Once they read the news they understood and we all shared the sadness of our loss.

As sad as I was over the loss I could not help but feel a sense of warmth and comfort in knowing that my family understood my sadness and tried their best to comfort me. They did not go about their business but instead sat with me and let me know that it was OK for me to be sad.

Humans are very complicated. Understanding their desires, trying to accommodate their emotions and assessing their level of knowledge can be a lifetime task for us in the animal kingdom. Actually, I think that humans have the same complicated relationship with each other. If there is one area where I feel totally confident in generalizing human behavior is that humans complicate life.

CHAPTER 5

"The better you know yourself, the better your relationship with the rest of the world"

Toni Collette

CHAPTER 5

So many people get pets and have no clue why or what they are doing. Now that may sound harsh and I am not suggesting that all humans are this way. Like I said earlier, I try very hard not to generalize. However, just look at how many groups have been formed to take in stray or abused animals because the people that had them decided that they no longer wanted them.

It is disgusting on how wide spread this egregious behavior is. I think humans have a tendency to act first and think about the repercussions later. My sense is that this behavior is not unique to topic at hand.

I guess some people feel like they can just discard anything they get tired of. This crosses all aspects of their lives. It is no wonder there are so many unhappy and discontent humans.

Perhaps if humans took the time to understand why they want an animal in their life there would be fewer adoption centers. More importantly, fewer animals would have to be put down.

So I would like to offer a little counsel in this area. Perhaps before you leap into "owning a pet " (I hate this phrase) you should do a little analysis. Think about your life style and you as a person.

When my family was looking to buy a boat the man asked many questions. He wanted to know what they were going to use the boat for and how often they thought they would be out on the boat. At the time, I thought what difference does it make they want a boat. I realized later that he was trying to make sure that they got a boat that was right for them.

First do you really want a "pet" as you human refer to us? I like to think of it as an addition to your life, a new member of your family. In my family I am like a son. I often hear "That's my boy" when referring to me. I do not feel like an asset or a pet. It is that feeling of belonging that establishes the attitude and behavior we bring into the relationship right from the start. Knowing you are a part of family makes the transition into a new home and environment much less traumatic.

The biggest question you need to address with yourself is whether you are really ready to make the commitment that having one of us in your life requires? Think of it this way, would you want a child in your life? Yes, I am comparing getting an animal with a human child.

The way I see it there are differences but in many ways introducing a pet into a household requires the same commitment as bringing home a new baby or a young child.

Routines change and the responsibility of caring for another puts a whole new dimension to ones own life. The point is that we need the same care and attention in our own way as a baby.

In a human controlled environment we are totally dependent on you. Unlike a child we will be dependent on you for life. Now let me add, I have observed on TV, many children remain dependent on their parents longer than the life expectancy of many in the animal kingdom. The point I am trying to make here is that we are a long-term commitment.

Another observation is that some humans tend to act compulsively without thinking through the ramifications of their actions. In their minds, it is like there is no downside for them. Sometimes on TV one can hear "we are a disposable society". Translated to me if it doesn't work get rid of it. Are humans really too busy to stop and think about decisions like adding a long-term commitment to their lives with a pet as if it is a pair of shoes that they decide they don't like.

I can't help but ask myself since humans have such a sophisticated intellect why they don't stop and think through their actions. Why do they have to make so many thoughtless decisions? I know that I keep repeating that I am not referring to all humans but there is a very large number that fit this profile.

I must admit this human trait has bothered me for a very long time and I have spent a great deal of time trying to understand this behavior and come up with some rationale for this behavior.

I guess the only answer I could come up with is that most humans don't take the time to know and be honest with themselves. They make their decisions based on what either they perceive is expected of them or what the current rage is at the time. I just don't know why humans tend to act in such a compulsive manner.

I find it very sad for humans to think they have to be something they are not. I have been made aware there are many books on human behavior and many theories. Humans live in a very complicated world much of which they create themselves. I feel that many choose a lifestyle that adds the unnecessary confusion and so the most attractive option in their decision process is to take the easy way out. How ironic that for the most part, the perceived easy way out more often than not turns out to be the most complicated.

So if at this point you are wondering why I, a dog, would entertain this line of thinking the answer is actually quite simple. We spend our existence unconditionally loving and trying to meet your needs. So to do our job we need to understand human behavior. In other words, we need to know what makes you tick. Many of us myself included see this as our job and our purpose in life.

I will go out on a limb here and ask how many of other humans in your life take the time and effort to truly get to know you and try to understand your needs. If you are honest there are probably not many. In fact, I will venture even further out on that limb and suggest that you yourself do not take the time to truly get know yourself.

Can you imagine what your life would be like if you and every other human took the time to become who you truly are and not what you think you have to be in this world. But I think we all are aware that is not human nature.

Over the years I have witnessed many changes in how people treat not only themselves but each other. I have grappled with this concept called values and how the change in values has impacted human behavior. More importantly, how the change affects human relations with us non-humans.

CHAPTER 6

"Try not to become a man of success but rather try to become a man of values"

Albert Einstein

CHAPTER 6

A major observation that I have made over the years is that humans pay homage to success. Once again I have to admit I have had a difficult time understanding the concept of success. I kept asking myself what is this thing called success and why do humans strive for success. The other underlying human behavior I thought might be related to success is the values humans live by.

Now I am the first to confess both of these topics are over my head. I had a terrible time sorting out what if any connection the two had with each other and how either impacted my relationship with humans. Needless to say I had a lot of questions. Here I had to rely on either my life experiences, what I have gleaned from television and my family.

There may be some of you at this point who are wondering why I would even broach this subject. My answer is quite simply that to try to understand these concepts enables us to better understand how best to maximize our integration into the lives of the people we live and in some cases work with.

The logical starting point for me was to ask is success in and of itself a bad thing or is success a good thing. In the animal kingdom is there this concept of success? I had lots of questions to sort out in my mind.

I do think we in the animal kingdom strive to successfully complete a task and when we do there is a sense of pride. I never get tired of being told " Good Boy" or getting a high five (which I can do) upon achieving whatever task I was suppose to complete. It is even better when I do something out of the ordinary totally unexpected and my family or others are in complete awe of my accomplishment. I have watched on TV rescue dogs that are given awards for their valor and the look of pride is unmistakable.

So I have concluded that we in the canine world do strive for success. Our behavior is driven for the most part in trying to please our family or handlers. However, we are not driven by success as it appears many humans are. We do not start out saying my goal is to be successful. For us success is the outcome of an act or task. Success is not our main goal. Doing our job is the main goal and if we do it well we are acknowledged for a job well done and for us that is success.

I speak for myself when I say that completing a task successfully and being rewarded for it gives me the confidence to do more or try things that have more risks associated with it. My experience with humans is that many humans do not have success as their main goal but rather the outcome of their stated goal or objective as well.

I have come to the conclusion that success in and of itself can be a good thing if it is achieved honestly and for a good purpose. As I pondered this question of whether success is a good thing or not I found that if success is achieved in a less than honest way and not for the greater good, it can be very detrimental to the achiever and in some cases to humans in general.

So what makes success good or detrimental to one's self and to others? In developing my thoughts I asked myself why in some instances one's success is another's disaster. I recalled that during the disastrous events surrounding 9/11there were some people celebrating the attack. I could not understand why anyone would celebrate that kind of behavior. For those that carried out that despicable task it was a success. They had achieved their goal.

In my eyes this was not good success because it was not achieved for the greater good. However, from their perspective it was a success because they had caused harm to the enemy. We happened to be the enemy. The light bulb in my head went off. It is not success that defines a person but rather the values one manages his or her life. Different humans have different values.

One thing I have observed over the years is that the way people interact and treat each other has changed. I watched a show that discussed how much human values have changed. I am guessing that there is a connection between how people interact and their values.

I have to admit that this concept has been very difficult for me to understand. I am not sure that I get it. My sense is that one's values are basically what one stands for and how one lives his or her life. Now if this is close to the case then values have indeed changed over the years in my humble opinion.

It seems to me that from what I can glean from the TV that people have lost respect for each other. In my family we seldom even listen to this thing humans call the news anymore. There seems to be so much violence in the world and I think a lot of it stems from the lack of respect people have for each other and their things. Respect is a virtue that I feel is essential to living in harmony with each other.

So why you are probably wondering is a dog so concerned about how humans interact and their values. Again my answer to that is quite simple because we in the animal kingdom share this planet with you and what you do to each other has a direct impact on us.

This concept of human values has been top of mine for me. It seems to me to be the glue that determines the kind world we all live in.

Perhaps that is why I feel so strongly about sharing my thoughts and perspectives. It seems to me that if one could put aside one's total focus on one's self and consider the impact of one's actions on another, more often than not a different action would most likely take place.

If respect played a greater role in how we value others and how we value our environment and how we value ourselves in our day to day lives then in my humble opinion this planet would be a much more beautiful and peaceful place to live.

I couldn't help but wonder if the world was ever simpler and more importantly a place where people held respect for each other in the highest regard and if so was the world a more harmonious place.

My sense is that there was probably a simpler time and that people valued others differently than today. If I may so bold as to say and probably in a more respectful manner. But no matter how far one would go back in time there would always be this overriding thing called "greed" that overshadows everything. It seems to me to be the driving force of the conflict that we experience in our lives.

If I could make one wish I think it would be that humans be more respectful and greed not be the driving force that it is on this planet.

CHAPTER 7

"There is a sufficiency in the world for man's need but not for man's greed"

Mahatma Gandhi

CHAPTER 7

I know that at this point most of you are shaking your head and thinking this stuff is not coming from a dog. I sometimes ask myself why I am I thinking of things like why are humans obsessed with things and what is this thing call greed all about.

At my age I lie in my bed and these are the kind of thoughts I contemplate. I wish I knew why I am like this but I do not have answers only questions.

I keep asking myself why. Why is taking care of one's need not sufficient. Once again, I have to say that this does not apply to all humans. I have watched documentaries where there are humans that do not have sufficient food or shelter to sustain a healthy life.

These people and there are many people on this planet in this category are not driven by greed. For the most part they simply want to sustain life. I guess this resonates with me because in the animal kingdom the battles we fight are more for survival and protecting our space. So as I sort out the question, I have to acknowledge greed does not drive everyone. The issue as I see it however is that everyone is affected by someone's greed.

So it begs the question are humans happier if they have more than what they need to survive. Quite frankly, from what I can tell the answer is not really. Let's look at what having more than one requires can result in.

Let's start with food. Anyone watching TV or just walking down the street has to realize that obesity is a major problem affecting the health of a large number of people in the US and in many other parts of the world. The health issues are serious and in many ways life threatening. Heart disease and diabetes are among the largest and the only one that benefits from this is the Pharmaceutical Companies. I figured this out watching the hundreds of drug commercials. Quite frankly I hate the commercials that tell you to take this pill or that pill and it was solve the problem. Even I a mere canine know that is not the case.

Another prime example is one's living arrangement. I am not suggesting that one doesn't need a place to live. The question is what is sufficient for shelter. Like food do we really need a big house or more than one residence. If one has a large family than a big house can be justified. The question is does having a large or fancy house with bells and whistles make you happier or more fulfilled. Like too much food does having all the extras just lend to more costs and issues with things breaking down and needing to be fixed.

Now this hits home. In my family we have more than one house and as I transmit these thoughts I am getting a very curious look. I think I have hit a nerve with my scribe. However, the look and thoughts that I am sensing is this is your book and your perspective, so keep on transmitting. So I will.

Do more clothes really make people happy or feel fulfilled. There are some humans that truly believe more makes them happy or at least they think it makes them happy. I think that they are kidding themselves. These material things that they think are so important are merely masking their unhappiness in my humble canine opinion.

Anyone watching entertainment shows that exploit the lives of the rich and famous can surely see how superficial their lives appear to be. Do you really think these people are happy? I would suggest they are not. Because in the same shows that exploit their glamorous lives there is often a dreadful story on the dark side of their lives.

How often do we hear about the over dose of drugs or worse their suicide. Divorce is a common topic on these shows or in the news. Even on the news, which I rarely get to watch because it is rarely on our TV, one hears about this important person or another going to this thing called "Rehab". I am not sure I understand what Rehab is but it does not sound fun. Now does that kind of lifestyle sound happy to you? It doesn't to me. I definitely prefer a simple uncomplicated life.

It seems like no matter where one turns greed is a major driving force behind the ails of human life. When watching the documentary about the puppy mill it was greed that made the people resort to the abusive and criminal behavior. Turn on the TV and there is case after case of greed driving human behavior. It seems that humans never have enough.

I think this concept of needing more is what drives the desire to be successful and unfortunately greed. Some humans say it is "human nature". I say it is the reason that there are so many unhappy humans. I do not think having more makes one happier. I feel strongly that one finds happiness in oneself.

In the animal kingdom, if our basic needs are met we are normally satisfied. For us food, shelter and procreation are our major concerns. Having never lived in the wild I can just go by what I have learned from TV and what I need in my daily life. However, as being part of a human family I do not care if we have one house or three, I am happy as long as my needs are met and I am with my family. My motto is "a simple life can lead to a happy life".

So that raises the questions of why many people find comfort and peace with animals in their lives. What is the old saying that "dog is man's best friend" because the dog or in many cases horses, cats or whatever animal species is driven by the desire to please and never asks for more than the need for them to sustain life and comfort the human that they are entrusted to take care of.

Our values are more in line with the values I think many humans wish existed in their lives. This recognition seems to be appearing more and more and in many different ways. Perhaps in some subliminal way humans sense that all of the material things that they have accumulated do not give them the happiness or fulfillment they strive for. Maybe they feel best or happiest while grooming their horse or sitting and petting their cat or dog. Maybe it is the connection with their best four-legged friend that truly fulfills them.

I do feel that some humans are beginning to more and more appreciate how having an animal in ones life can make a difference. Perhaps it is because we in the animal kingdom have not been all caught up in this greed thing or its evil partner power.

CHAPTER 8

"The day the power of love overrules the love of power, the world will know peace"

Jimi Hendrix

CHAPTER 8

The question I have been asking myself is what are the drivers that derail a human being from truly achieving fulfillment. By now you know my opinion on greed but right there with greed is the insatiable quest for power.

I guess I need to define the kind of power that I closely align with greed. Just like success, power used in positive ways can be a good force. For instance having "will power" is a good thing. The Power that I am describing is the power to take advantage of another. My sense is that it has existed as long as humans and perhaps those of us in the animal kingdom have existed.

Now I have to admit that we in the animal kingdom have our own issues with power. We have our pecking order in the pack and there are battles often times that determine the Alpha member in the community. I use the word battle because that is usually what ensues for the right to dominate.

I think the same exists for humans. One can look around and see the quest for power everywhere. It dominates the world. Countries are frequently referred to as "World Powers".

The powerful are held in high esteem and also feared. It is those that are held in fear that are the most concerning and destructive.

In my opinion every war is driven by greed and power and at the end of the day one has to ask what good was achieved. Isn't there another way to achieve the objective at hand than to wage a war? The answer of course is yes but the simple fact is that greed and a quest for power drive the path to war.

This to me is the underlying or fundamental flaw in human behavior. Having said that I have to say not all humans are driven by these unflattering traits. I say that because my life and how I view human behavior has only been slightly tainted by this phenomenon. Fortunately, there is a balance by humans that offset this bad behavior

We can only hope that this balance continues and that greed and power do not totally take over the planet.

Once again I have to ask whether one that has this insatiable thirst for power ever really finds true fulfillment in the power that is achieved. Is the cost along the way worth the prize in the end? If I venture a guess I would say the answer more often than not is NO.

I personally have not been impacted by power but I have witness others that have and it is not a pretty sight and more importantly can be terrifying to those that suffer from those that abuse power.

The world without power and greed would be a wonderful place to live. Don't you agree?

The sooner that humans realize that greed and power do not lead to happiness the sooner humans can find the right path to happiness.

CHAPTER 9

"There is only one happiness in this life, to love and be loved"

George Sand

CHAPTER 9

I think humans strive to be happy. Their biggest problem is more often than not they do not know what true happiness is. I stated it earlier and I will state it again humans complicate life. This complication not only clouds the definition of happiness it totally distorts it.

I had to ask myself, why for humans does everything have to be commercialized. Happiness in my opinion can be achieved in many ways. Those of us that have experienced true happiness realize that it has nothing to do with gifts. It has nothing to do with what you have or what you have achieved. From where I sit there is a big difference between being happy and experiencing true happiness.

Like most everything in human society, happiness and love are commercialized. Humans even have a holiday called Valentines Day. On Valentines Day one is supposed to give the one they love a present. I think one should let the people they love know every day in some small way that they love them. The gift could make them happy but no commercial gift will give anyone true happiness.

Now don't get me wrong, anyone who knows me knows that I love to get presents. I trained my family early on that presents made me a happy boy. However, having said that it isn't the present that brought happiness but the gesture of giving something because that person cared enough to share something special. The gift made me happy. It did not give me true happiness.

For me my true happiness is experienced everyday as I give my unconditional love to my family and friends. It is what fulfills my life. If I did not have the life that I have I sometimes wonder if I would have ever experienced the greatest gift in this life and that is true happiness.

In the animal world we can experience happiness in a very uncomplicated way. We are not faced with same stimuli that humans have in their day–to-day lives. In many ways we are shielded and are able to keep life and therefore happiness simple. For me true happiness is to love and to be loved and I have been blessed to be able to love and experience love in return.

Humans are bombarded with the commercialization of what makes one happy. It consumes their everyday life. TV ads are the worst. But it is much more than just TV it is everywhere one turns. This will make you happy or that will make you happy is the message that transcends one's external stimuli. There is so much external noise it is difficult to find peace and introspection in today's world.

For me finding a quiet place to contemplate fulfills me and gives me joy. My family usually left the TV on for me and I did watch when the program that was on piqued my attention. But many times I just went to another room that was quiet rested and found peace. As I said earlier for me watching a sunset at the beach is Nirvana. True happiness is a special gift that everyone can achieve and doesn't cost a thing.

My perspective on happiness is the one gift that I hope I have imparted on my family during my time with them. This is particularly true for the type-A in the family.

One of the first books read to me was the "Little Prince". The first time I did not understand 99.9% of it but over the years with many readings to me I began to understand the true meaning of the book. The point I am trying to make is best stated in this book by the fox when he gives the Little Prince his secret and says to him "It is only with the heart that one can see rightly; what is essential is invisible to the eye".

I cannot put it any more beautifully, simply or clearly than that quote and if this canine can get it then any human that takes the time to read and think about it can better understand this secret to a happy life.

CHAPTER 10

"The Essence of all religions is One. Only their approaches are different"

Mahatma Gandhi

CHAPTER 10

It seems to me that human's quest for finding peace, harmony and happiness takes many different forms. Some forms like material wealth and celebrity in my opinion never achieve the happiness that they are trying to achieve. One form of searching is this thing called religion. From what I have gathered there are many different religions. This concept as with many that one confronts living in a human controlled world is very complicated and not one that as far as I know exist in the animal kingdom.

One of my first questions early on was does religion affect human behavior and if so how does it? This question is important because if there is a significant affect of religion on human behavior the next question is how does that affect the relationship between the human species and the animal kingdom.

Every year for as long as I can remember my family would take me to be blessed on a certain day each year. For me as a puppy it was just another outing. There were all kinds of animals and usually one man although I did remember a woman once or twice that would say some words and sometimes sprinkle some water on each of us. I was told I was blessed whatever that meant. I did not feel any different and there were no treats so what did being blessed mean.

As I got older I went to my human go to person and asked about this event that we went to each year. It was the first time the concept of religion was explained to me. Once again, I listened but did not understand the explanation. This concept was so foreign to me that I knew that it would take a great deal of time to understand this part of life with humans.

In addition to being blessed once a year, I would accompany my family to their religious services when they were held in an outdoor venue. A man would speak to them and they would sometimes answer and there was music and people would sing and sometimes my family would sing along as well. The people were friendly and I noticed that the same rites were performed each time I was in attendance.

Over time I began to get the gist of the concept of religion. I am the first to admit that I still do not understand many of the teachings in the different religions but one thing that I have ascertained is that many humans find a deep need or guidance in finding an inner peace and an understanding of life. In many ways religion provides a roadmap or guideline that shapes the values they hold onto throughout their lives.

The one underlying theme in most religions seems to be that there is One that is greater than all others, that is beyond being human. This One has the power to enlighten and guide humans in their search for true fulfillment.

Now once again, many of you are shaking your head and saying no way this canine is writing this stuff. While I am not writing it per se I am transmitting my thoughts to a scribe that is putting the words on paper. Lest I remind you that dog spelled back words is GOD. And yes, I do know that many believe in God as the One. It is terribly important for those of us that have to live in a world where there are many humans that practice many different religions to better understand how religion affects our relationship with humans.

This concept of Religion is important for many reasons. Many would say that it is the underlying fabric of human behavior. It is one of the things that make humans superior to all others.

I have been told that I am getting into a topic that is so complex that there is no one unequivocal answer. I am not trying to answer questions that have not been answered for thousands of years. There is no way I would feel the least bit qualified to even attempt such an exercise.

I am merely trying to determine the extent that religion no matter which religion affects human behavior and the interaction with the animal kingdom. Perhaps this too is a question that has yet to be answered or perhaps there is no one answer. In any event, the question at least gives us the opportunity to pause and think about how one's belief affects our relationships with each other no matter the species.

When I asked about the event that I attended each year, I was told that it was the blessing of the animals and that it was typically held on the feast of St. Francis of Assisi. I liked that there was a special blessing for animals even though I did not know exactly what that meant.

So I asked what is a blessing and who is St. Francis of Assisi. After a rather lengthy explanation this event that I had no real connection in my early days became for me a special time with my family. I paid more attention to the words that were said and had a greater respect for the ceremony itself. For me it was a way that some humans took the time to bring their non-human family and friends to participate in a rite that was special to them

I recalled sitting on the bed with my nanny, (that is what her grandchildren and therefore I called her). She would tell me that she was saying her prayers and that she prayed for her family and for me. I did not know what that meant as a puppy but as I got older and after she passed on I realized it was her way of letting me know how important I was to her. She wanted the One that she believed in to take care of me. She did not just seek fulfillment for herself but more importantly for her family and that included me.

I guess you could say I found my answer to how religion practiced by humans affects their relation to the animal kingdom. So I was glad that I asked the question even though there is probably no one answer. I felt a great deal of comfort and at my age this is terribly important.

CHAPTER 11

"An awareness of one's mortality can lead you to wake up and live an authentic meaningful life

"

Bernie Siegel

CHAPTER 11

As I was finishing up my memoir, I realized that I spent a fair amount of time lately thinking about what happens in this period often referred to as the after life.

This was vey top of mind for me as this year at my birthday for the first time my two best buddies would not be there to celebrate with me. Quite frankly I was in a funk.

I became more aware of my mortality. As with my buddies and many others in my life that had left us I began to question what happens to me. What happened to those that are no longer here?

As with many things in life the answers come in different forms. If one is open to receiving answers in unusual ways the answers can be most meaningful.

For me, it was going to see my buddies' mom when I got back to the town where they had lived. I did not want to go. Let's say I had to be persuaded by my family. In other words I had no choice on this one.

Not only did we go to a different house, there was a new member of the family. A dog named Sam. I was in sensory and emotional overload. I could not wait to leave as much as I love my buddies' mom.

I had a myriad of questions going through my mind. Is this what happens when someone near and dear to humans passes on? Would my family forget me and just move on? What becomes of me? I have to admit I went from being in a funk to being downright depressed.

The only way to deal with my state of mind was to try to find the answers to my questions. I went to my go to Human for some insight on the matter. The response that I received was very thought provoking.

Like the questions I had about religion there is no one answer to my question. Since I was asking a human, I received a human's perspective. I was told that humans handle death in many ways. Everyone is different. One way to look at death is that we are all energy in a physical shell. I am in a dog shell and my family is in human shells. When we pass the shell is gone but not the energy.

I started to think about that explanation and it made sense to me. I reflected on some of my life experiences and came to believe that somehow my energy would always be with my family and theirs with me. I was no longer depressed about the future.

That was one human perspective but I was told there were many. This perspective worked for me because it was simple. In the animal kingdom we keep life and death simple.

Humans on the other hand tend to complicate things. So for me it was simple there really is no death. There is the shedding of the physical shell but the energy lives on.

Humans on the other hand tend to complicate life. Therefore for me the question became do humans reflect on mortality? And if so how does that reflection impact their behavior.

Reflecting on the question, I recalled an experience I had with a very close friend of our family. I was lying in bed with her one night and she was petting me and telling me how lucky my family was to have me in their lives. She was very sick and I think she was reflecting on her mortality.

All the things that seemed so important to her before were now immaterial. She felt that she was lucky to have the time to pursue what was truly important in life. She cried and hugged me and I stayed very close to her that entire night.

We spent time with this special lady and I did see that knowing her time was limited made her a more authentic person. All the material trappings did not mean a thing in the end.

In the end she like so many of us are reminded that the quote from the "Little Prince" is what truly matters. " It is only with the heart that one can see rightly; what is essential is invisible to the eye"

It was one of her favorite books and it is also one of mine.

If we could all live with that philosophy life would be simpler and more meaningful. More importantly, wouldn't it be great if we all became aware of our mortality very early on in our lives and live our lives like there was no tomorrow.

CHAPTER 12

"Generally I tend to despise human behavior rather than human creatures"

Sidney Portier

CHAPTER 12

So for those readers that have gotten this far, I thought I would leave you with a few thoughts to reflect on and hopefully appreciate what I have tried to share in this exercise with you.

I feel fortunate to have lived in a human controlled world. I have been able to experience the good and observe the bad in the world. So I felt that since I have had a privileged life and the ability and opportunity to transmit my thoughts that it would be a mistake not to.

Some may think that I feel that all human behavior is bad. That is by no means the case. I have seen unbelievable love and kindness by humans towards other humans and to the animal kingdom in my life. I have tried to point out the human kindness and the ability of humans to care for each other and those of us in the animal kingdom.

In my 17 years (that is old in dog years) I have known unconditional love from my family and friends. I have seen that humans with their unquestionable intellectual capabilities change their opinions and more importantly their behavior. Sometimes the change is for the good and unfortunately sometimes for the bad.

There are many in the animal kingdom with similar observations about human behavior to those that I have discussed. We all, for the most, part live in a human controlled world. Even those of us that live in the wild are subject to the actions of humans. Like I said earlier we all share this planet. What you do to each other affect us as much as how you treat us.

A main point that I have tried to convey is that there is no need to complicate life. The more complicated one make one's life the less likely to find true happiness. The drivers of life's complications are for the most part created by you.

If we keep it simple then it is going to be easier to find the answers. Many humans have come to understand and try to communicate this rationale in many ways. The perplexing question is why more do not adopt this philosophy.

It just seems that most people are trying to find peace and happiness. Unfortunately the complicated materialistic world that they've created distracts them from finding true happiness. All the glitter and noise over shadow the peace one finds on a quiet beach at sunset or looking at the sky from a mountaintop and seeing all the stars in the sky.

If one finds happiness in a simple life then one is not as inclined to fall in the "greed" trap. The need for more of everything at any cost doesn't exist. They have found what they need in themselves and those they love and care about.

Another observation that I tried to convey was that we in the animal kingdom have a great deal to offer. Given the opportunity we can enhance one's life in any number of ways. Those that have embraced our talents have found fulfillment not found in any other relationship.

We have no agenda we just want to make you happy. Well to be honest sometimes we will be extra good to perhaps get an extra treat or two or to do one of our other favorite activities.

We like you are each individuals and we differ in what we like and what we are good at however the one overriding trait we all have is if treated kindly we will give unconditional love to those we cohabitate with.

We may differ in size and color and there are many different types of canines not to mention other species in the animal kingdom that share a special relationship with humans but it is important to note that the more you get to know us and appreciate what we have to offer the stronger we both will be in the end.

So the next time you are with one of us take the time to look into our eyes because we are probably communicating with you and letting you know how important you are. Take the time to talk to us and let us know how much you appreciate the relationship you have with us.

The more you communicate with us the more you will understand us and get a better understanding of what we are trying to convey. It would be great if we could speak a human language but we cannot. That is not to say we don't communicate. We do the best we can and try to get our message across in a simple honest no agenda way.

It is so important that you acknowledge our cues. Take us out when we need to go and not when it is convenient for you. It let's us know you care about us. It lets us know that you are trying to communicate with us, that you are trying to understand our needs like we try to understand yours. This is particularly important as we get older and need to tend to ourselves a bit more frequently or are more particular as to what we will or can eat.

The more that you incorporate us into your family and your lives I can pretty much guarantee a more fulfilling life for each of us. Just think how good you feel when we greet you all excited to see you and share our love. Make it two way street and let us know how excited you are to see us. Tell us how much you miss us because although we can't speak to you in your language we do understand it and like to hear you speak to us in a loving respectful way.

If someone asked me what the most important secrets to the success that I have with my family I would have to say that very early on I decided that my relationship with them had to be a two way street. It was really tough on both of us early on but boy did it pay off in the end.

The other major ingredient to our loving and fulfilling relationship is respect. I have to admit that I was always treated with respect and it goes without saying that I adore my family but as importantly I respect them immensely.

I have said it before and I will say it again these special ingredients to successful relationships are not only applicable to a relationship with the members of the animal kingdom, in my humble opinion are just as important to human relationships.

So as I end my perspective on human behavior I feel that if it gets just one human to rethink their relationship with the animal kingdom or better yet with each other then this exercise will have been not only worthwhile but successful.

Thank you for being open to a different perspective or at least a perspective from this genus Canis.

CHAPS

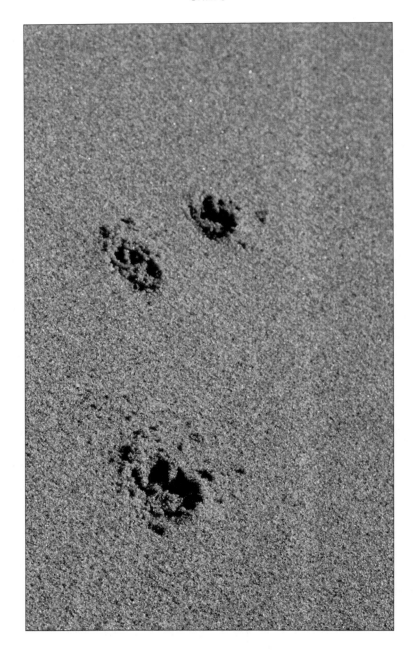

EPILOGUE

On March 17th 2001, unbeknownst to us at the time, our lives were about to change dramatically. A five-pound puppy we named Chaps with lots of energy and quite a bit of swagger marched into our lives and became a member of our family. Looking back he was the center of our universe for the seventeen years that he shared with us.

From the beginning, there was definitely something different about this puppy. He had presence and he let us know in no uncertain terms that he was going to have a say in the family.

While scribing for both of his books, I learned a lot about him and more importantly how he perceived the life and experiences he shared with us. There were many moments that I could not believe what I was typing.

On too many occasions I couldn't help but think is he referring to me and have I been so insensitive to him and the animal kingdom in general. Am I one of these not so nice humans? He had a way to make one stop, think and reflect.

I suspect that some that have taken the time to read his words will have a hard time convincing themselves that these are the thoughts of someone other than a human. Those who knew him and were a part of his life will have no doubt that this came directly from him.

I do not know how many times we were told that he wasn't a dog but a person in a dog body. Even one of his vets when discussing his care with an assistant said "He isn't a dog he is Chaps". Others would talk to him and he would look at them with his penetrating dark eyes and they would look up at us and say "I think he really understands what I am saying to him". After going through this exercise with him, I know he did know what they were saying and somehow over time he was able to put it all together. On one occasion a highly regard animal communicator described him as a "Little Buddha".

Chaps always the inquisitive one, would give us the look. His head cocked to one side, as if to say what does this mean. Sometimes the answer would satisfy him and he would walk off and lay in one of his beds and if one took the time could see he was absorbing the answer. If he didn't understand the answer he would just give you the "I don't get it" look and walk away and try again at a later time. He didn't give up until he got it.

From the beginning he was always engaged in life and learning and experiencing new things. There was no doubt when he liked something and when he didn't. Looking back he was always a great communicator and he demanded that we communicate with him.

For the over two years, I have scribed for him. It was not a task that I relished or took lightly. However, it was a task that in the end provided me with an incredible gift, one that I cherish.

I now look at sharing this planet with members of the animal kingdom with more respect. I have a better understanding and appreciate their intelligence and ability to enhance our lives. More importantly, I have compassion for their struggle to live in a world as Chaps would say "controlled by humans".

I better understand the principle of keeping things less complicated. And most importantly, he crystalized Antoine De Saint-Exupery's quote from the "Little Prince "what is essential is invisible to the eye".

He stated earlier, his mission in undertaking this project was to get just one person to rethink their relationship with the animal kingdom and with each other. If he could achieve that goal, he would consider it worthwhile and successful.

I am here to declare that his project is worthwhile and successful because this human has indeed reflected and changed how I think about my relationship with the animal kingdom and life.

Perhaps that was the purpose of the entire exercise and in effect the real purpose of his life with us was actually to make this human a better person.

Hopefully, others that read what he had to say will come away rethinking their cohabitation with the animal kingdom and with each other. Maybe he will have the same effect on them as he had with me that being a desire to be a better person.

On March 23, 2018, Chaps as he believed shed his dog shell. His physical presence is no longer with us but the impact he made on us and those he touched during the time he was with us will last forever.

Thanks Buddy

Your Scribe